What's the Score?

99 Poems

Also by David W. McFadden

What's the Score?
99 Poems

David W. McFadden

Mansfield Press

Library and Archives Canada Cataloguing in Publication

McFadden, David, 1940-
What's the score? / David W. McFadden.

Poems.
ISBN 978-1-894469-62-3

I. Title.

PS8525.F32W43 2012   C811'.54   C2012-900848-6

Editor for the press: Stuart Ross
Cover design: Marijke Friesen
Typesetting: Stuart Ross
Author photo: Max Middle

The publication of *What's the Score?* has been generously supported
by the Canada Council for the Arts and the Ontario Arts Council.

 Canada Council **Conseil des Arts**
for the Arts du Canada

 ONTARIO ARTS COUNCIL
CONSEIL DES ARTS DE L'ONTARIO

Mansfield Press Inc.
25 Mansfield Avenue, Toronto, Ontario, Canada M6J 2A9
Publisher: Denis De Klerck
www.mansfieldpress.net

*Dedicated with love
to Jennifer Celeste McFadden
of Hamilton, Ontario*

Contents

1. Stimulation Galore

Heavy winds and raining heavily though warm
this morning but this afternoon was sunny
and hot. Even the birds are singing with an
Italian accent. I'm in a tiny chapel
dedicated to a Madonna in 1580.

The mountains are dreams rising from the lake.
I lit a candle for luck in the church of St. Giacomo
where there's a thousand-year-old stone altar.
A marble life-size statue of Christ entombed.
The bull has a respectably long penis.

On the train a seventy-five-year-old man
wearing an excellent grey suit insisted
on having an elaborate conversation with me
in French all the way to Luxembourg.
He was a retired baker and a widower.

Poetry happens when language is used as a
device to broaden, deepen and intensify
the quality of emotion you are trying
to invoke in yourself. He showed me pictures
of his two children and five grandchildren.

He had no English but he recited beautifully
Rudyard Kipling's *If* in perfect French.
He got off at Brunelles and a tiny blond
grandma and her grandsons six and eight
got on and began giving me lessons in French.

They were going all the way to Como.
So when I got off I had lost all
my French and Italian and everything.
It's amazing how many people could not
muster up even one little word in English.

Not the station master or his personnel.
Not even the woman who sold tickets and cashed
my traveller's cheques. Not even bus drivers.
Not even the policeman who couldn't figure out
what to do with the fifty-year-old drunk.

The drunk was wearing a woman's dress and kept
pulling it up over his waist, exposing
nothing but his heavily stained trousers.
They didn't know what to charge him with
and everyone in the train began to shrug.

A beautiful woman came up to me and said,
"You are not a virgin and you have no child."
And then she said, "Let me be your child."
She lifted her dress and showed me a nasty bruise.
The bus to Bellagio had long ago gone.

I could hear the roaring waterfall
but couldn't see it no matter how I tried.
The men in the Bar Milano in Nesso
glanced at me but they didn't know
beans about the wonderful English language.

My complete and utter lack of Italian
was no laughing matter at the time.
In flashes Italian mountains made me feel
very peculiar. As if I had lived forever.
As if I knew infinitely more than I know.

Right under my window a boat goes by.
It's the *Ninfen* of Lake Como (the *Water Lily*).
It's full of school kids, teachers and parents.
They're all wearing sunglasses. They are
looking in different directions but not up here.

All you need to know about a salamander—
you don't need to know how fast it can run.
We can see how fast it can run. It's obvious
they run so fast when a human comes wandering
down the path because we are so scary.

The lizard will lie in the cool darkness
waiting for the distant sound of dissolving
humans. And then he will spring to life
in the sun, listen to the birds singing.
Most men only want to drink and hold forth.

There are about a hundred young people
in the launch sailing beneath my window.
They're looking out in the many directions.
Soon they'll be hiding behind the trees
but still not a one has noticed me.

Italians have an intimate relationship
with Lake Como, more than others have
with the Great Lakes. They love it and they
are like children around it all the time.
They're all over in all manner of boats.

Sailboats, powerboats, speedboats, hydroplanes,
tourist launches, magnificent yachts, canoes,
strangely shaped one-of-a-kind inventions,
new imports from Japan, and the people
in bathing suits are stretched out and sunning.

Or maybe slathering oil on each other.
They feel no need to make any pretense
that they are not enjoying themselves immensely.
They go around in circles or they reconnoitre
in the middle of the lake to exchange news.

Like their boats, they come in all shapes
and agedness, youth and amount of tan.
Are desires inspired by the gods or do
humans make a god of their desire?
Shall we swim in circles or straight lines?

By arming ourselves with a knowledge of temporalia
we must avoid succumbing to temptations.
This implies a conscious controlled descent
into the underworld in order to see
how little good exists in the world of the flesh.

We extricate ourselves from being trapped.
To learn about the nature of vice is a virtue.
This is the story of Orpheus and wisdom
and Eurydice and concupiscence or passion.
It's always fun to swim in circles and lines.

Or as truth is disguised in fiction
or as the truths of philosophy may be
disguised or veiled in poetry. This morning
about four I had an attack of aphasia.
In my dream nobody had any sympathy.

And today I had another look at what
is my favourite painting at the Serbelloni.
The conversion of Saint Paul. It was a Bembo.
And the same look on Paul's face was on
Saint Francis's face as he receives the stigmata.

Is it truly a Bonifacio Bembo?
I wonder if they realize that it is.
I think he never even signed his paintings.
David, you talk too much. Stop talking and listen.
Many men when they reach your age start drinking.

They drink too much and forget
to listen. All they want to do is drink.
Their writing suffers terribly and they die.
At Victoria Station I'll never forget
the golden filigree in your eyes.

"You're going to have to let go of him now."
Pure gold, the porter telling us to move
with a minute left from the window to the door.
But now a boy of fourteen puts out his nets.
He's dressed only in a pair of jeans.

He's in a silver splendid twelve-foot outboard.
He stands and moves the oars a bit then throws
out another length of net. He'll sell
his catch to the local *ristorantes*.
Or maybe to the people at the Villa.

Thank God I've forgotten my desire for perfection.
It was in my blood, then one day it left me.
This is the picture of the way I was.
Now it's the only way I am in poems.
Perfection—and then I don't give a damn.

Then there's a tale about a white elephant.
Every poet at times must wonder if he's
a victim of a plot. Baraballo
was an elderly priest from Gaeta
who thought his verses were products of genius.

Petrarch had been publicly crowned on the Capitol
and Baraballo thought he should be too.
Pope Leo X who loved a nasty joke
offered his beloved elephant, Hanno,
to Baraballo so he could have a ride.

He rode from the Vatican to the Capitol,
dressed in a scarlet toga fringed with gold.
And to the sound of ninety-seven trumpets.
Hanno was a present from King Manuel
of Portugal—but Hanno became frightened.

Hanno stood trumpeting before the bridge
of Saint Angelo and refused to move.
Was it the shouts and cheers that frightened him?
Maybe the stench of the rotten corpses
that hanged from the gibbets of the castle.

We're told that elephants are highly sensitive.
The daily average was fourteen executions.
Maybe Hanno understood more deeply
and refused to go through with his role.
As for Leo, he thought he was a poet.

Chaucer visited Florence to check it out
and was told the Presbytery was the oldest
building in the world and he believed it.
I saw three paintings of the Virgin
in Mennagio, each with a sword in her hand.

On the western shore of the northern arm
of Lake Como everywhere I went
I carried a candle and thought about the saints
and their sufferings and innocence.
My suffering is negligible, believe me.

Whatever I get is more than I deserve.
No big deal but I wish I knew where you were
and I could up and go there straightaway.
Knock on your door, tell you how moved I was
by all those little golden sparkling tears.

Red flowers to the Virgin of Montserrat.
Portrayed *con bambino*. Jesus a golden saw,
with sawtooth mountains above the lake.
Below me the Italians scream with pleasure
as they go by in their little boats.

From now on I think I'll believe in God.
So many people refuse to believe.
Maybe they do but then pretend they don't.
Believing in God, believing you and me,
God believing all of us constantly.

Being bathed in the light of consciousness.
Never judging us but always the urge
to become beautiful and perfect.
This thought is born out of despair
into something easier to cherish.

2. Trapped in a Snake's Body

The void of intelligence is the Everlasting.
We all know there's only one religion.
I saw a snake today and I wasn't
in my pajamas for the heat.
I was wearing my best suit and tie.

I felt myself trapped in a snake's body.
I felt myself trapped in my own body.
I felt a flash of fear as it slithered.
Jennifer called just before dinner.
My daughter wants to come to Italy.

After all, she's broken up with her boyfriend.
She feels guilty but he's got a new one.
She's decided she wants out of Hamilton.
She's not going to where she thought she'd go.
Her first crack at tennis and she's fast.

It's my game, she says. Better than jogging
and even better than weightlifting. What I
want to do for the rest of my life.
Read, write, play tennis, look at paintings.
È Bellagio un villagio?

A vulgar person calls you a nasty word?
Remember that in Italy the word means "ace."
"The nice thing is that even if mother
says I can't go I'm going anyway.
I love her but she's held me back a lot."

Dear Ann is using spray cans to paint
cloud formations. She's the Tornado Girl.
She hasn't heard of the greenhouse effect.
Dear Jane is great but I think she doesn't
like anything about her Italian husband.

Jane admits that philosophically
she considers herself a neoplatonist.
She's doing for medieval literature
what Erwin Panofsky did for painting.
I'm busy listening to my Italian tapes.

The morning sun is sparkling on the water
four hundred feet below, with a couple of kites
gathering string and twigs, and soaring in circles.
They'll be active in the afternoon,
building a nest to the left, behind the trees.

A little smile, friends, that's the thing.
Thinking of Jenny flying across the Atlantic!
She's also in that poem "Low Tide at Grand Pré."
When Rochester says "Mister Benny" he's saying
"Mi sta bene" which means "it fits me well."

I'm standing here watching birds this morning,
watching the humble wrens, gulls and the occasional
soaring kite with twigs. It's not the count,
the lists or the identification.
It's entering their strange little world.

It's quiet and you can hear the falling leaves
and the subtle shaking of the ground
or tiny silent movements of the snakes.
The lizard stubs its nose into my foot,
then he scampers up my naked leg.

A kite squawks thrice and then it sleeps.
A badger waddles through a patch of hillside
and stops to take a leak. A great red star
quiet as an early memory has moved
up over the outlined mountain peak.

You say too much in a poem and all the
poetry is gone! Gulls bark like furious
little overweight but mellifluous dogs.
Each little light on the far shore
has a tongue sticking out across the lake.

The star above the mountain is still red
(and still still) but the sky's beginning
to turn a pale blue. My handwriting
improves as the sky continues to lighten.
I lost what I wrote on that slip of paper.

A freight train goes by on the other side
and enters the tubular tunnel on the way
south to Como. Or is it the Transalpino
from Brussels via Lucerne, Metz and Strasbourg.
I'm waiting for the sky to enlighten me.

If I turned on the light the dark would vanish
and the room would fill with moths and bats.
I could close the windows but it's too hot.
Please, no screens—the atmosphere would ruin
the perfect sixteenth-century atmosphere.

The songbirds are all awake and belting
out their cosmic symphonies. I stick
my head over the railing and whistle a song
in imitation of a wren on the branch.
That shuts him up for the rest of the morning.

Oh God! What a genetic monstrosity
of a wretched wren nesting in that chapel.
On the rock, fifty feet below,
over the days a purple flower has bloomed.
Haven't been working on my Italian lessons.

The Leaning Tower, the Baptistery, the Duomo—
and it's pretty well time to go home.
I went to the Cappella Medici—
a glorious mausoleum for the families.
The guides are bad. Repetitive, not appealing.

Pisa enjoys for centuries an uninterrupted
flow of tourists. And such a small city.
Someone wrote that no one goes to Florence—
no one is interested in Renaissance painting.
I found the place cool and free of tourists.

The frescos were very mysterious.
Got a nice snap of a Pisan trattoria
with a waiter dressed up like the Leaning Tower.
Last night at the station with Jennifer—
very strange and moving. She was wonderful.

It was an archetypal situation.
Daughter leaving alone for Greece and leaving
father teary-eyed in Florence after
a week together. We only had an hour
so I taught her the cardinal and ordinal numbers.

We talked about the necessity of being
in the moment (the key to everything)
and how it is fundamentally different
from "living *for* the moment." It was such
a lovely time with the sun going down.

When the train came it seemed to be full
of men waiting to pounce on her! Of course
San Gimignano would be lovely at night—
in the winter—but in summer full of tourists
it's a bore except for the frescos of Niccoló.

Tourists are masters of feigned nonchalance.
The main thing that has changed for centuries
in this landscape is the speed one can
traverse it. Twice this week I've been
accused of being a thief. Before, never!

With this guide everything is either famous,
typical or important. Monteriggione—
Dante's giants on the hill, halfway
between Siena and San Gimignano.
Beautiful. Interesting. Must stop later.

Life is as short as it is beautiful.
Love is even shorter and more beautiful.
If everyone who ever committed suicide
out of youthful despair could instead
have merely visited Italia!

Saint Catherine of Siena's head on display
is in a side altar of San Domenico.
Brown, shrunken and with a strange smile
(lopsided and somehow intelligent).
Brown as my shoes, the size of a baby's fist.

One poor child has had a sword enter
his mouth and come out at the back.
Two saints were hanged and are being stoned
by eight soldiers. Their bodies slashed severely,
while their pale faces were left untouched.

I'm lighting a candle for my friends. My function
is to light a candle and pray. Why not?
A curious painting in the Mangia in Siena.
The town hall. No one knows anything about it.
It's not labelled and it's not in the books.

Even the local art experts pretend
to never have heard of it. A massacre
of the innocents? Complex interplay
of characters, not faded at all—
but early Renaissance, no perspective.

There are castles in the mist. It's raining hard.
We're on the train to Rome but we change
at Arezzo for one hour for Assisi.
We're going through tunnels and the windows are open
for the humidity. Dark curtains blow.

I want to be a saint like Saint Francis.
That is why I'm practising being in the
terrible terror-filled moment and deeply
immersed in the history surrounding us.
Everything becomes charged with importance.

Goodbye to Florence, again I was accused
of being a thief. Guido and Gabriella
told me I had to move to a smaller room.
I refused and when Gabriella insisted
I accused her of double booking. She relented.

The next night a woman of a family from
North Carolina pointed at me and said,
"He's the reason we couldn't get our room."
You can have tons of fun at the Rigatti Hotel.
Didn't get to see the Museo Archeologico.

Anything can happen. The corn is tall
and the sunflowers are turning their heads.
In the middle of a cornfield, a square
of mausoleums with an empty space
in the middle. A city of the dead.

Everything's so beautiful, it's almost
unbearable. One must stoutly resist
fleeing into the past and/or the future.
Travelling through Italy by train
on a rainy afternoon in August.

Resist like a knight facing a dragon
crawling up on his horse's hind leg.
My hand makes shadows as I write.
Saint Catherine holds out her hand to Christ
and she is handing him her heart at last.

Climbing up to Assisi and the Basilica
matches Glastonbury climbing up the Tor.
It seems a place designed to breed saints.
Can't seem to squeeze enough time for the writing.
The tomb of Saint Francis and the Giotto frescoes.

To live in the moment with all one's might
eclipses all our spiritual exercises.
When Jesus offers his parables he says
paradise no longer needs to suffer.
Just throw yourself away, that's all you need.

In the Basilica the light from the chapel
seemed to probe and penetrate into darkness.

3. Scream in High Park

I wore this T-shirt all day today
and it's amazing the number of people
who came up to me and said hey man
how come you're wearing that T-shirt
with today's date on it? None.

4. Kirk Douglas Walking along Phipps Street on a Sunny Afternoon

My name is Kirk Douglas and I'm in love
with the blond, blue-eyed Doris Day
and the dark, mysterious Lauren Bacall.

Doris's desire is to make me happy,
Lauren loves to drive me out of my skull.
It makes more sense to stick with Doris.

But when I get a call from Lauren Bacall
I remember the strange women of Dublin dressed
in black and carrying bouquets of white roses.

5. Windy Afternoon on Elsewhere Street

Frantic the way this little row of trees
is waving its branches around. The energy
of youth—they're only eight years old
and it's obvious they'd like to be elsewhere.
Somewhere in the country maybe, where
they can listen to each other's secret thoughts.

6. Friendly Waitress

The big baseball game was on TV.
Last game of the World Series.
Me: What's the score?
She: I don't know. I have no interest in sports.
Me: It must be a pain having customers
ask you all the time what's the score.
She: Yeah it is, I never know.
Me: Just tell them 5-5.
She: That's a good idea.

Now whenever I go in there I say
what's the score and she laughs and says 5-5.

7. Rebecca's Sweet

She says just tell the receptionist Rebecca
says it's quite okay to ask for her.
It's a code. These women love their codes.
They're wildly interested in each other.
And so they should be. They are all so different—
unlike men who are pretty well the same.
I wonder if Rebecca's sweet on me.

But I look very prosperous in my new
hat made from coconut fibre and
with the wildest dark green band of silk.
Plus in my eyes there's a mischievous glint
that says to any woman looking for something
I know you're different from all the other girls
and I'd love to find out in every way.

8. Cinema Darkened

For hours we were sitting in a darkened
cinema arguing loudly and bitterly
and all the other seats were occupied
with sheep and cows and horses and pigs and ducks.
On the screen was *Young Man with a Horn*.

I was at a point where it was feasible
to take my life and flick it out the window,
go somewhere where no one would ever know me,
take up mescal under some volcano where
I could master the doctrine of No Mind.

You were saying what a great idea! You've
got my blessings, what are you waiting for?
And all the animals were politely silent
but I was arguing—I wanted to stay
where I was and wait for miracles.

Everything was terribly unpleasant
especially when you said I should go now
because pretty soon you were going to come down
with something requiring chemotherapy and
I've never found the sick all that attractive.

9. Point Seizure

The doctors insisted there'd be no more seizures.
But the next day you had the worst of them all
when they had the bronchoscope down your throat.

We phoned Bobby and he began to howl
like a ghost, a knife pressed to its throat.
We'll have to get some help for that poor fellow.

He says we shouldn't pray for you because
that's the occult and don't we read the Bible?
That book says we shouldn't practise magic.

The worst was when you were in the shower,
when you collapsed and cracked your head on the floor.

10. Passion for Life

The French say if you do your nails
on Monday you'll be healthy.
The Greeks say if you do your nails
on Tuesday you'll be wealthy.
I am neither French nor Greek
so I thought hard for a week.
I tossed and turned all night long
wondering if I was right or wrong.
Then one day I said hurray—
I'll do my right hand on Monday
and my left hand on Tuesday.
I felt as clever as a fox.

That was thirty years ago.
Today I'm healthy as an ox
and I'm rich as Michelangelo!

11. Poem Beginning with a Line by Horace

Many have perished who trusted too much in their strength.
Many have perished who trusted too much in their wit.
Many have rusted who trusted too much in their thrust.

It's wrong to dismiss an artist on moral grounds.
Those with spotless records in that regard
simply have not disclosed the total story.

Shall we refuse to read Mallarmé because
his family paid to keep him out of the army
or because he greeted his father's death with a joke?

There's a difference between someone who's dying
and someone who is dead. Take Baudelaire—
despised and tormented all his life
but at his funeral declared a genius! Unfair!

Of course it's unfair too that Mallarmé
said he couldn't tell one *anglais*
from another. But there'll be another day.

Only a nincompoop would hold that against him
and use it as an excuse to avoid his verse.

12. Enlightenment

Gardening and photography, his hobbies,
went together like old age and death.

I understood when he grew tired and gave
his Leica to his sticky-fingered son.

But when he committed to the flames his entire
collection of slides of glorious dahlias

that he'd cultivated over a lifetime
and flowers of all kinds from around the district

or from botanical gardens around the world—
I looked into his eyes and asked him why.

"No one was interested." Tears appeared.
This was in his early seventies.

He had several years left of growing flowers
but they blossomed and faded unphotographable.

13. Gogol's Dogs

Some remedies for boredom: you can dance,
you can play some instrument, and you
can also get married and/or travel.
After writing this I decided
not to put hot sauce on my trout.

We were going over to Ward's Island
and got on the wrong ferry by mistake.
It was the Caribana Weekend Reggae Cruise.
For three hours Margaret Hollingsworth
and I sailed around the harbour helplessly.

We drank beer and ate chicken and rice
and even though we were the type to prefer
Mozart to Marley we danced wildly.
A psychiatrist from New York said she was
having a good time but not a great time.

She looked a lot like a black skin Katherine Hepburn.
We poets can't afford not to eat
(when it's free). (Put on a different coat,
and you're a different man.) She said
she was about to enter her sixth decade.

Next day I was the guest of dishonour
at a dinner hosted by Gogol himself.
I had one piece of meat on my plate.
He said, "Look here, everybody needs a mate,"
and plunked a second piece down on my plate.

Then he said, "Two is of the devil.
Let's make it a trinity," and with that
he plunked down a third. "Have you ever
seen a house with just three corners?"
and he plunked down a fourth ad nauseum.

"I can't eat another mouthful," I insisted.
He said, "There was also no room in the church,
but when the mayor showed up *they* found room."
And he tossed another T-bone on my plate.
This is the way it goes when you're on a roll.

Gogol was so ugly one suspects
when he said so-and-so had a face
like a badly baked loaf of bread
he was talking about himself. For a party
trick he'd cover his nose with his lower lip.

And he'd take a sniff of his own bad breath.
"Civil servants are a queer lot,"
he'd say, "as are people of other professions."
He possessed a great number of dogs:
for instance, Shoot, Swear, Dash and Fire.

And then there was Bully, Blast and Plague.
Scorcher, Hurry, Darling and Reward.
Also Guardian. All twelve of them
put their paws on Nozdryov's shoulders
at the same time. Can you imagine?

Then Swear went over and licked Chichikov
on the mouth, obliging him to spit.
In a letter to a melancholy friend
Gogol said: "Everything in the world
is arranged in a most wonderful way.

"The gay will instantly turn to sadness—
if you dwell on it then goodness only
knows what ideas may not come."
Suggestions: If you haven't got time
to read Gogol please make sure at least

you read the first two paragraphs of chapter
six. And for dessert, the last paragraph
of the same chapter, and then
why don't you try to have a little nap.
And dream of some remedies for boredom.

14. Morning Star Rats

Some poet, I can't even tell you how
sad I am, how I hate being here
but don't want to be anywhere else,
how I can feel eternity in my spine
but I've got the weariest headache
and my nose is full of dust because—
well, never mind why because—

Friends call at the wrong moment
and I snap at them and then I call
back in an hour to apologize.

Evening approaches and yet still we hear
the Morning Star patiently calling.
Who dares to care if everyone I know
is planning to winter in Morocco?
Strange the way it doesn't bother me
that I'm stuck in Canada for the winter
(though last-minute miracles aren't unknown).
Geographical location lacks significance
in the face of the dreams I've been having,
the dreams of vultures circling overhead
and trying to get into my window where
I sit drinking tea and eating something
with strange elation and total absence of fear.

15. The Vine Comedy

When your body dies and your spirit
is finally free after all those years
of imprisonment in solitary confinement
you find yourself confronted by a trio
of guardian angels, friendly guys, so they say
(they being the Neo-Theosophists and so on),
and these angels invite you to watch
a slow-motion replay of your life
and they help you (if you need help) to discover
where you went wrong and where you went right,
where you learned the lessons you were intended
to learn—and where you just plain failed.

And they help you plan the perfect next
life for you, one that will not punish you
for your sins exactly, but will give you
(how to put this now?) a greater opportunity
to learn the lessons you failed to learn this time
(for instance you might become a sea slug).

So far in this life in spite of numerous
opportunities I don't seem to have learned
much about love and I'm seldom seen at
the food bank helping the poor and lost get fed.
Somehow it's just not in me but I'm not
a cruel person, overly, ordinarily.

Now I'm thinking there's a possibility
I might be in trouble for not having taken
the time to appreciate the work of Cézanne,
also I've been overly fond of randomness.

And then I've never been able to get past
the first part of *The Divine Comedy*
(a fact that could cause me deep regrets
in another world I sincerely hope is better).

16. Two Strange Things She Did

Once while visiting my studio she grabbed
a bottle of my whisky and took a big slug
(just put it to her lips and sucked it down)
and continued to talk as if nothing had happened.

Once while walking through posh Rosedale,
she started pawing through some garbage that had been
left out for a ritual collection.
Then she just got up and continued walking.

In both cases, given the nature of her being,
the actions were entirely out of character.
In both cases it was as if she was extremely
conscious and unconscious of what she was doing.

In both cases I detected faint smiles
but I could have been somewhat mistaken.
I filed the events away with no comment.
And somehow I think she knew I did.

17. Nothing at All

Sometimes I think if I had a real job
I'd have to go on leave for a number of months
to get over whatever it is that is
making me want to die. Other times
I think if I had a real job I wouldn't
want to die I'd just be dead. My brain
is split in two, one side wants me to
run towards you, and the other away.

The desire to die lacks a will to die,
the desire to live lacks a will to live,
and there is no death or life these days—
only an envy of those who have gone before
and a sorrow for those who haven't arrived.

See all this hair on my face? This is what
happens to men when they lose the will to shave.
It's as simple as snowflakes. When paralysis
strikes we decide to do nothing at all.

18. Dolly

When we see a silhouette we don't know
if it is really there or a cut-out
of what used to be there—until we go
up and touch it, but even then
we might not know if it is there or not,
and if it is there perhaps it is not
intended to be seen as having been there.

The first mammal has been cloned. A sheep
strangely named Dolly, a name that connotes
unreal, not alive, a mannikin,
an imitation of life, something that can
be toyed with, exploited without mercy.
Does Dolly feel different? Does she bear
a mute and glorious wound that won't disappear?

When she is with other sheep does she know
that she's somehow not of the same order?
Now we can clone humans, but that might
not be necessary, why not just
clone a sheep with the intelligence
of an Einstein? Or an Einstein
with the intelligence of a sheep?

The human race is coming along in a hurry.
For years we've known of the inevitability
of the cloning of mammals, but only now
with Dolly gazing out at us from every
TV screen do we realize we've entered
a scary scenario—Torvald Helmer
totally ignorant of his wife's warnings
that she is going to leave him, and now
she has left him and he's overwhelmed.

19. Ode to Gustav Meyrink

Impressionable too, an angelic presence.
I have a friend who claims when he was young
I visited him when he was in a book shop
and insisted he buy a copy of *The Golem*
(by Gustav Meyrink) which he duly did.

And as he read he recognized the voice
of the author as that of the angel
still using the powers at his command
to get people to talk about his books
though it's hard to imagine a bonafide
angel worrying about my funny friend.

But wait a moment maybe it was merely
my friend's golem or exteriorized self
(his better half?) for after all it's known
we are more likely to experience
such things in senility or adolescence.

And it's known that Meyrink when he was
a troubled youth got ahold of a loaded gun
and was about to put a bullet in his brain
when someone slipped a flyer under his door
advertising a new book called *The Hereafter*.

Said event caused him to put his gun away
and to study the occult for the rest of his life.
His moral conduct was always questionable.
(He even ridiculed the military.)
But when *The Golem* was published in 1915
Meyrink became famous but then he died.

20. A Year in the Life

Heaven, I'm in heaven!
I've got a hot girlfriend who's only twenty-seven!

Hell's gate, I'm at hell's gate,
I got a faithless wench who's only twenty-eight!

The moon, like a mouldy mushroom cap—
and all the truly
great ideas you're not
going to hear spoken.
They go so fast.
Yes they go by far too fast to turn them into words.

21. A Shower with Sharon

Old and poor were her clothes
but she knew how to wear them.
She was handsome, tall and calm,
and she wore a black silk scarf
and she had a beautiful repose.

"Don't be so obsessed with your hair,"
(she said to me) causing everyone
on the patio of Ted's Bar to turn and laugh.
What about all that fun we had in the
shower that time? Sharon, I'm sorry.
I know what I did and I didn't do it.

22. Blessed Bond of Board and Bed

Wally got entangled with another woman.
His wife put up with it for a while
but when she told him to leave finally
he hanged himself on the monkey bars
and left her and the kids without a dime.

Wally's wife had a strange memory trait:
she could remember every word
from every song in all of Shakespeare
but she couldn't remember a single line
from any one of the most famous speeches.

Wally's wife used to tell Wally he
should be living by himself on Hornby Island
writing the same poem over and over.

23. Written on the Sand

To die a dozen deaths a day is the fate
of those overloaded with fear.
To battle huge waves in a tiny boat
is the fate of those who receive love
in excessive or inadequate measures.

We'll be grey before the ring's on our finger
or the halo afloat above our head.
We want to die but we're not ready,
or we're ready to die but we don't want to.

Why does so little happen each day?
Of course we experience the same thing
over and over, of course we're surrounded
by ghosts and guardian angels, all subject
to the eternal laws of eternal recurrence.

We long to be kidnapped by flying saucers
and to meet tourists from the thirtieth century.
We're genetically programmed to lie on the beach,
and when we're tanned we could print on the sand
in letters straight and long and hot and hard....

MY GUIDING ANGEL GUIDE TO ME MY LIFE
OF PURPOSE THAT SERVES MY HIGHER SELF

*P.S. The letters had been stamped out on the north shore of
Lake Superior on a completely vast and isolated stretch of sand.*

24. Heartburst

I've been coming here for many years
and I don't even know your name.
Nevertheless I've taken your advice:
I get a manicure every week.
Now that everyone dresses alike
a flash of the nails reveals one's class.

There are many moments out of time
when your heart will burst and form in your hands
a cup to catch the arc of your blood.
And also too in a moment out of time
there's really nothing we can do
to save anyone except ourselves.

For you and I have arrived at a place
from which we can never return,
a point in history where we make a pact
to exist as blameless as a fart.

25. Everyman Youthful

Many of us find ourselves planting
one foot in front of the other.
We're all the same but some of us
have overly developed editing skills.

It's not necessary to admire or envy
the special talents for life some possess.
Win or lose, rich or poor, we still
breathe in and then we breathe out.

In my dreams a smiling old man
with only a few little lines on his face
tells me over and over again
until he's sure I've got it straight

that his name is "Everyman Youthful."
In the morning the sun has a strangely
self-important look on its face:
the old boy's bright as blazes as he
unbuttons his creamy coat of mist.

26. Haydn Sikh

Why do we do things anyway?
Isn't it enough to sit and stare
and maybe weave a little web or two?

All the time we used to talk about
free will and myths of eternal return.
I can't remember which side we took
but we'd get steamed up and twist and shout.
Come on outside and see the garden.

The spiders have died of overconsumption
or maybe of the summer's fiery heat.
Their webs are full of dead mosquitoes
and the sun doesn't miss the slightest trick
(it points its nose at every little thing
and its reflection ripples across
the liquid ripples of the lake).

The sun doesn't seem to mind if it's
seldom worshipped anymore. The Mayans
would scoop up sacrificial blood
and flick it at a hovering Venus—
but we New Age folks merely flick
the sun's reflection back at the sun.

27. The Lady of the Lilacs

We bicker and quarrel and don't seem to have
any discernible patterns to our lives.
We're all riddled with secret and shameful
desires impossible to acknowledge.
We move about forever in awkward spurts
of sexual display and savoir faire,
gathering tropes to help us maintain
the pyramids of our primacy.

But the lady of the lilacs has gone to seed
among the rain barrels and greenish weeds.
The lady of the lilacs has gone to tell
the Sleeping Beauty it's time to wake up
and join with her in serenely awaiting
the final extinction of all we hold dear.

28. Knot a Poem

During Prohibition a quart of Canadian
gin fetched twelve bucks in Chicago.
The true poem only deals in facts.

How could I have anything to say
to anyone? The power of these
mighty verses, which will never appeal
to anyone but those who are keeping cool
while the world falls apart all around us,
comes from that refusal to fall apart
about which nothing can be spoken.

Each word is a leaf on a tree,
or maybe a valley, or a hill, or a river,
or a portrait of that gardener at Arles.
Oh to be flecked in soot instead of a
character in *The Metamorphosis*
or some poor suitor of Penelope
radiant in her brand-new business suit.

29. A Life of Loneliness

The very young and the very old
laugh when reality blows up in their face.
By this time tomorrow every transformer
in the entire county will have exploded
with power-line extensions like rattlers
causing creeks to boil and roads to crack.
Hills we never knew were volcanic
are giving birth to litters of lava.
Bodies are falling from the sky
and landing in the unlikeliest places.

Hip hip hooray it's judgement day!
You can't force people to take an interest
in whatever it is you happen to be doing.
You continue on and take humble pride
in not being annoyed when your friends
yawn when you talk about your dreams
or don't notice the irises in your vase.

It's a lonely life and thank heaven for that.
You wonder what your former friends are doing
and where former friends are forever going.
You rejoice when the dumber ones get rich
even as you're dropped from their party list.
Quietly, not caring if you understand,
which of course you do—perfectly.

30. Ghosts

One's knees stop shaking about the time
childhood friends are retiring from
their carefree and sensible careers.
While you learn to talk like a chorus girl
and even to dress and to think like one.

You learn to love your furry loneliness
and the boredom of keeping your ego afloat.
You can't go back, you can only drift.
Hereinafter called the artist as it
used to say in dusty old contracts.

A ghost came up to me and he didn't
seem very pleased to see me there.
He thought I would have gone by now.
He asked me in his iciest tone:
Still here? Why haven't you gone?

His opinion of me wasn't good.
In no way was I the sort of guy
he'd be if he were flesh and blood.
He wouldn't be sitting around like me
reading books and sometimes writing poems.

But everybody's so nice, they seldom say
you're a wastrel and a parasite.

31. Roman Candle

There was a moon with a man in it
and since we seemed to be in the sticks—
backdrop after backdrop of stars!
Our planet has a lovely point of view.

I had an awful dream last night. I dreamt
blood gushing from a little wound.
The harder I pressed the higher up
into the air the blood would zoom.
Doctors and ordinary folk
seemed to think it was a joke.
They oohed and awed to see it spurt
but they seemed to think I wasn't hurt.

The staff of all the clinics in our town
refused to look me up or even down.
I pressed and pressed and the blood shot high.
I thought for sure I was going to die.
But normal people taking the evening air
picked their teeth and simply didn't care.

Cataclysm is overdue.
Fresh blood has a fiery glow.
It's very much like an active volcano.

32. Funny Country

In a funny country with no name
the dead are embalmed in such a way
they keep as fresh as a fallen log.

The living carry them here and there
to picnics or to the cricket match
and they engage them in dialogue.

In this lovely little land success
is all that folks are left with when
they don't try hard enough to fail.

Success goes hand in hand with shame
but failure has a nobler sort of name.
Success is something to condemn.

For it makes a fool of them and it
chokes them in their dark and dirty sleep.
Failure's grand and it's hard and deep.

33. Favourite Philosophers

My birth trauma was so profound
my life has been a merry-go-round.
I study and scheme and try to be
as cheerful as the sweetest buttercup.
But when I'm down I'm too far down
And when I'm up I'm too far up.

Last night as I lay in my bed
of all the people alive or dead
Humphrey Bogart came into my dream.
We were sitting in a little café.
He was relaxed, not at all mean,
a bit chubby, with a nice toupée.

On the wall was a mural I loved
but someone was painting another one
on top of it and that ticked me off.
Bogie smiled and he looked at me.
He was trying to tell me I was wrong
to worry about some stupid painting.

"Under the aspect of eternity,"
he said, "it doesn't matter, don't you see?
In my time I was a great
admirer of Spinoza, mate.
But," he added, "my favourite dames
were those who favoured William James."

34. Circuit-Breaker

Everybody wants everybody
to see the purity of their heart—
but everyone has all the purity
he or she or it can handle already.

So when somebody says how do you do
the other never says: "Sorry, I'm not
taking personal questions today."
One is much more likely to say:
"Top o' the world!" or "Never better!"

Everybody in the world is working
at the important job of taking energy
out of the world and putting it back.
Employment is close to a hundred percent.
And fate, the will of the planet perhaps,
has reserved numerous efficient ways
of killing off those who break the circuits.

How old is the universe anyway?
    Chorus: "Really really old!"
And where is the universe exactly?
    Chorus: "You're standing right in it."
What if there were no universe?
    Chorus: "That's a tough one, like
what do you mean by 'universe' anyway?"

I get the point. I like you guys. Stick
around, everyone should have a chorus
following his steps and reminding him
of his central role in some great dream.

35. Solemn Atmospherics

Sometimes an average guy will say something
a bit too loud and a bit too dumb
and everyone will turn around and give me
a nasty irritated look my way.

Look at me, I've always been a thorn
in your side since our first meeting
at Sandy's soirée in seventy-seven.
I think it's time to leave if I can.

Yes of course it's time for me to go.
You can stay, don't worry about me.
I'm off to find another Nevada standstill,
hopefully half my age and twice my height.

Will you itch for the touch of my thorn
as much as you used to all along?
I see myself at the end of every street
waving like mad for you to hurry on.

Invisible comedian of language:
solemn of tone and with atmospherics.
That's what I get for not having lunch
with you, Sandy, last Saturday.

I'm not saying I'm going to wait until
you call me at a time when I'm at home.
"For personal reasons, I've resigned."
(A peaceable sort of suicide note?)

You asked last night where I bought you that
chocolate bar that was so delicious.
Why don't you come up and ring my bell
with flowers and wine at some perfect time.

36. Miles Davis

It's not how rich we are, it's how rich
we feel we are that really counts.
No way I'm afraid of waking up
and discovering my so-called poverty,
or my self-satisfied indolence
amid my hereditary holdings,
curiously loathe to honour the dead.

So here I am recovering from a horror!
An accident on the road! The capacity
for suffering so deep I never knew.

Swollen hearts and even broken livers
float down bitterly from the sky.
"I never wanted that gig anyway,"
Miles Davis said when he had his crash.

I'm always strangely proud that I've resisted
the pleas of certain moneyed folk
to come and live with them in Etobicoke.

I suppose you wanted out of me exactly
what I wanted from you. Needed: A lot
of laughter and a certain freedom from want.

37. That Melanoma on Your Left Wrist

I know it's taken me far too long
to come to terms with the depths of love.
A pair or two of popular styles of living:
torturing oneself and torturing others.

It's still amazing how I found you floating
downstream in a hot pot of mushrooms
then bobbing up and down in the weeds
and I took you home to cook and clean
over and over every second day
with your eyes staring into mine
coldly but with flashes of warmth.

A chocolate wrapper flying in the mist,
that melanoma on your left wrist,
the lama loves all those heartfelt sutras.
And though it's sometimes hard to figure out
how to love what we can't understand
that needn't stop me, for I could never
love any code already deciphered.

In order for me to become a saint
I'd have to live in a land of lamas.
A paramour is a thing of nought
said Bolingbroke or some other sot.
The greatest sadnesses are forever those
that'll make us look back with a silly smile.

We never recover from the milder sort.
We live our lives with a sword in our heart
but a bolt from the blue can really smart.

38. Bottom's Dream Shoes

Why did it take so long to settle in?
Already the buzzards are drowning
the carcass of our love. Who knows?
When we die we'll be a butterfly.

I was bottomless, you were marvellous
to tell me so, though I felt like Bottom.
You were semi-awkward, tall and thin
but you nearly gave my heart a spin.

Then it stopped and then reversed itself
that time when I realized again
instead of being glad to see me back
you were overjoyed to see my back.

I thought I'd been struck with an axe
but it was nothing but a scratch.
And if today heaven came to call
I'd tell the angels that I gave it all.

39. Molecular Equation

He's the guy whose radio broke down.
He checked the television. It was all right,
the waves on the beach, the wind from the trees
and various voices from the street—

He could hear them all perfectly well.
He could even hear the old church bell.
But he got in his car and drove like hell
to the doctor's office to have his ears checked.

You're the woman who loved her cats so much
when your mother died you gathered up
all your morphine tablets in the cabinet.
When she was alive you'd never touch them.

And shortly thereafter the cat got sick
so sick it seemed ready to die—
you'd given it one of those tablets
(those veterinarians charged far too much).

So without much ado, or so I've heard,
the cat toppled over on its final purr.
You had that cat made from its lovely fur
(and from its skin a lovely hat, monsieur).

40. Hyacinths and Primroses

Life is but a bridge of dreams and yet
we're always making a huge fuss of it
and we often leave a terrible mess.

I know why, it's because it's more
fun than lying in bed all day
meditating on meaninglessness.

Three guardian angels came to me
and invited me to sit and watch
a slow-motion video of my life

starting with the moonlit night my mother
conceived me and ending with my sweet
inconceivable little death I guess.

I told them this was truly premature.
They said it was cool to be dead
and they were here to help me assess

how and why and when I'd made mistakes
while living my long and lovely life.
They were nice (in fact too nice, I thought).

So I told them about my dear old pop,
the news of my death would break his heart.
They closed their eyes and let me slip

back into my body, and through my lip.
There was all this ebbing ecstasy
and you were smiling up at me.

41. November Nightmare Bagel

Evening approaches yet still we hear
the Morning Star patiently calling.
A whispering kind of call it is:
"Serenity, serenity, serenity."

Who cares if everyone you know
is spending the winter in Mexico?
Don't let it bother you that you're stuck
up here in all this frozen guck.

It's already November and earlier
I dropped my bagel—and a squirrel
ran with it up the nearest tree.
The bagel was hot, fresh from the oven.

And what a treat it was going to be.
But the squirrel took a leap and its weight
caused him to miss the branch and hit
the sidewalk with a sickening scrunch.

Another squirrel scooped up the lunch
and ran in front of a tourist bus.
A baked good, only an hour old,
had already caused the death of two squirrels.

And that bloody bagel was good as new.
I picked it up and gave it a big chew
and continued along the avenue.
A pair of vultures hove into view.

42. Government Report

Years ago I realized I could
put anything at all in a poem,
no one would read it anyway
even if published in a prestigious
magazine or anthology.

The name of the author and the title
of the poem might have been noticed
but as for the contents I could take
a paragraph from a blood-curdling
story by, say, Crad Kilodney,
add a few lines from a government
report, and nobody would give a damn.

But then I slipped up, I wrote a poem
about an eighteen-year-old, a female Holden
Caulfield who gave me an interview
about several things she liked to do
and how terribly much she loved to screw.

In the poem she vividly confessed
the details of her wild sex life
and that was about it. Unfortunately
I gave the poem a title that caused
certain people to become disgusted
and I was close to getting busted
as a pederast for having written
"Sex with an Eighteen-Year-Old."

In fact my lovely publishers,
a married couple with kids of their own,
received stern condemnation themselves.
But no one gave the slightest hint

that they'd ever bothered to read the poem
for if they had they would have known
none of us deserved the guillotine.
It was just the girl telling the world
what it was like to be a teen.

43. The Ambrose Bierce of the Tokyo Grill

Who's the Canadian version of Roger Ramjet?
What's the worst thing about having a heart attack?
Who's the Grandma Moses of Nova Scotia?
Where's the fractured tennis loop of Africa?
Where do you go to come down with a code?

We went to Disneyland and who should we see
enjoying themselves: Jesus Christ and the
Twelve Disciples. There were no apparent
discipline problems. People were
ignoring them. But Mickey Mouse accidentally
bumped into Saint John and became
cross but he just said, "Watch where you're going."

Who's the Uncle Tom of poetry?
Who's the Glenn Gould of stamp collectors?
Who's the Billie Holiday of the five-and-ten?
Who was first to cheer when beer got dear?
The big thing is not to have death surprise you.

A.Y. Jackson dies and Saint Peter
at the Golden Gate says, "Come this way.
We have a lovely landscape and a box
of paints for you. This won't be so bad."

44. Aunt Sally

Nothing's true. Everything's mythical.
The imagination feeds on wormy corpses
then soars into the air above Death Valley.
Don't want people to look? Don't dress funny,
and all you have to say is something smart.

I know, I'm funny, and I can't help it,
but I don't have a warped sense of humour
(at least in my opinion I hasten to add),
this is the way we all were in my family
going back to the massacre of the McFaddens.

The great thing about waking up is that
we never know where we are for a bit
(one of the few moments of ecstasy).
Who knows where that avenue would lead us?
I opened the hood and the seals were leaking.

Did Flipper have a Zipper or vice versa?
We seldom think of seals having a leak.
You never know what astronomical problems
of definition one might encounter.
Such problems can be debilitating.

It's far nobler to read than to write,
and this is basically why I called you
to be with me today, my sons and daughters,
out here among the blossoms and leaves.
The masses of huddled crocuses a-trembling.

I try to be flirtatious in my poems
but it's boring to be flirtatious all alone.
I avoid advertising my mental states,
my sexual preference (flippers with zippers)
or my tastes in matters suicidal.

A gentleman never desires to draw
undue attention to himself.
But you were on my mind all day and I
wished you would have invited me to your party.
What day was it and what kind of guy am I?

I would have brought flowers, flowers and flowers
and would have been happy to show you all
my flippers and zippers and maybe a nipper.
I'd be happy to deliver your graduation
address and I'm being totally sincere.

I have a thousand picky things to deal with
and of course the sweetest smile so they say.
But one goes to the movie one goes to see.
Except that one never knows how much
intelligence one should bring to the film.

We prefer to rate films by the number
of three-syllable words that will fit
in every hot dog sold in the stadium.
Why not? That would frighten off the riff-raff
that wouldn't know a movie from a book.

I hate it when the tensions start running
and some bozo with no pants on yells,
"Kill the bitch!" And so I go over
and say, "Okay which one of youse guys
yelled that?" And one monster grabs me

and says, "What's it to you, queer?" And I,
so clever and quick-witted when lesser
mortals would panic, cunningly
simply compliment him on his "refreshing"
sense of humour. And pretty soon he's my friend.

How do some people manage to think
about anything but their own selves?
Egoless egomaniacs seek reassurance
with their gentle, pleading eyes which say
would you mind terribly much if I

(Aunt Sally) were to hop up on your lap?
Remember the day you said your name
was a rose by any other train?
Remember the night you said my life
was passing through your mind? What a song.

There are certain things you do only once.
Recall the day someone you can't remember
whispered in your ear, "There are no absolutes"?
I said there are absolutes everywhere.
You said, "No there's not, not even in grammar."

When one will let one's mind wander
one often encounters sources of discomfort.
But strangely enough one feels detached.
That's what they all say when you feel
your heart falling apart—you can't stop laughing.

If I were to fall at your feet,
would you notice traces of lust in the
boardrooms of your heart? You know we share
the deepest taste for the absurdities
of partial belief, belief and non-belief.

I don't mind mental patients, they're addictive.
As long as they're nice. Like, I don't mind—
if you're nice you can get away with anything.
This stupid old fool has become stagestruck
as if he didn't have gravy on his tie.

But he feels that special sense of sadness
and repressed anger. Everyone's got it.
Such problems. Mine are so small I have to
pounce and blow them up like balloons.
You don't have to explain, I understand.

You don't have to get out your violin
whenever I try to say how a year ago,
I wanted certain people to adore me.
Now when they declare their adoration,
I don't believe it. It's so much baloney.

Actually life has been very wonderful
except for that nasty Winnipeg Flood.
I'm still as lusty as ever. Rub it in.
My actions are cheap and my words are dear.
You can't have one without the other.

What would the world be like without me?
If I had any booze in the house I'd go
to bed right now. One of these days I shall
e-mail you this poem and it will take
its archival place in the cyberspace.

The old dream of writing the Bhagavad Gita
on an elephant's tusk and lo and behold
the elephant is doing Elvis imitations.
Our craving for attention and repulsion
will be amusing when higher species find us.

Remember that night we spent moonbathing
on Long Beach or maybe it was Short?
It's a lonely life for a man who has
to do what a man has to do, and that's
what I do—along with everyone.

45. Can't Get Much Closer Than That

Stock phrase among sports announcers:
I wish I hadn't told you to call me back
and tell me the story of Ivanhoe
because now I'm going to have to stay
awake when I'm tired from reading Proust.

In the small bar at the Delta Chelsea
it's too many peanuts and Heinekins.
Oh no, it wasn't Proust, it was Jean Rhys
about a seven-year-old girl who falls
in love with a man who wakes up after he dies.

They live in Dominica and they have a painting
of Napoleon's soldiers trudging through
the snow in the retreat from Moscow.
There's Dominica where Jean Rhys was born
and the Dominican Republic where I'm bound.

Maybe for the month of December to watch
summer sports. And there's Kick 'em Jenny,
an island I want to take my daughter to
(but Jenny's too old to go with her dad).
If only we didn't feel so much at home.

It's terribly awful but we still like it.
Of course I'm far too old to adopt a child
or even a smaller island of my own.
It's amazing how later I'm still thinking
about you when I'm thinking about anything.

One day I love you and the next I don't.
I love you and you love me, and it's lucky
I have no regard for my ego (in theory)
and I just look on in wonder and try to
imagine what I'd be doing if I was doing it.

I never think the same obsessive thought.
But then again for all I really know
pretty well nobody ever does.
A simple little thought can be obsessive.
Then there's the thought of a thousand thoughts.

We only have one thought from cradle to grave.
Nothing like a full moon to remind you
it's best to be sympathetic to the weak
and woebegone of the world. That's
everyone—on my block anyway.

I love it when people compliment me
as long as it's not all that sincere.
I hope I've said everything I have to say
and I'm finishing off this poem but quite
frankly I'm not the fanatic that I was.

The important thing is to write poems
and it doesn't matter if they're good or bad
or if they're for now or forever.
All the best poets seldom blot lines
but you'd never know it to look at them.

Time is going at the perfect speed
which is basically no real speed at all.
All day I've been devoid of desire.
When I succeed in living forever
it'll be time to wither and to die.

46. Fast Forward

So that was fun. Let's do it again sometime.
My new book: *Remember Me in Your Will*.
The bionic man is made of metal parts.
If you want me to I'll live forever
but if you don't at least remember me.

You're feeling full of something, I can tell,
that *bonjour tristesse* feeling slowly taking
its time fading out. I'm sitting and watching
several Buddhists watching the angry clouds
sinking into the sea of forgot-my-ticket.

Disappearance of tremendous turmoil
helps to ease the frustration of your fading
like a version of Ionesco's *The Chairs*.
We were planning to perform it one more time
but we couldn't agree on why we should bother.

So we decided to do some other play
in a sort of mime that quadruples
the speed of the thing. Call it *Fast Forward*.
I loved it but I never understood it.
Two poets, and one with a guitar.

We took turns singing a series of poems
all about unsavoury subjects.
We also did a poem of forgetfulness.
All our lost dreams, where have they gone?
Maybe they've all gone to the lost and found.

47. Cold Heart

From gutter to gutter, a leaf the wind blew.
You were sometimes cold around the heart.
When we were young we paddled upstream.
Now its better to paddle all the way down.

Smoking is a resistance to cosmologies.
Afternoon approaches yet still we hear
the Morning Star gently calling.
And the Evening Star does the same.

48. Rock Bottom

Never fuse with your muse and cast
a cold fish on love and hate.
Unless of course you want to lose
your marbles and your darling sweetie pie.
Fire and brimstone's not that bad.

Every day volunteers are welcome.
You'll find forms under every seat.
Fill them out—you'll be glad you did.
Blasphemy has never been my style
and the worst nightmare's only another dream.

No matter how bad it gets it'll be
good for every soul to be thrust
beyond every million years or so
into the red-hot centre of whatever
by simple design or impurely pure.

Which would you prefer, my daring darling?
Speaking hypothetically of course.
And after the credits in *Casablanca*,
Simon McParadise shouted, "Crazy bastard!"
I don't know why he did, he just did.

That way it's easier to be mysterious.
Charles Olson, for instance, used to bang
his bottle of Cutty Sark against the table.
Just an everyday point below the pint
where it would easily open straightaway.

49. True Nobility of Spirit

"What mixed a certain pleasure with my pain was
that I knew it to be a tiny fragment of universal love."
—Marcel Proust

You know when you're walking home at night
the ground is covered with severed hands.
Human hands sticking out of the grass
like tulips—and the forefinger of each
is pointing at you, needing a manicure.

Also sometimes the ground will be covered
with asparagus stalks sticking up in the air.
Or it will be covered with nocturnal robins
each pulling an earthworm out of its hole.
No reason for being alarmed. End of stanza.

Now you're imagining extravagant parking lots
with pairs of red lights going into the ground
all night long below that apartment building
at the corner of Bay and Saint Joseph where a
gastroenterologist was stabbed to death.

It's one of those nights you say to yourself,
I was wrong, I was hard-nosed, I didn't
want to take my half of the blame and any
sense of humour I'd ever had deserted me.
True nobility of spirit is inconsolable.

My prayer is to die, if I must, laughing.
You could make it yours too, my friend.
It lies in crying for the pain of others
and laughing at your own no matter what.
Don't be afraid to talk. I hear everything.

Even though I have no way of responding
still your busy signal is in sync with my heart.
I've never been very fond of surprises
unless of course it's me who's surprising you.
But I don't know if you're hearing anything.

50. It's Spring Again

It's spring, almost May, if I may
look at this phenomenon from a purely
egocentric point of view, one redolent
(if not too terribly immodest) of
everything we love down through the years—

Three sixteen-year-old girls neatly dressed
in air-cadet uniforms and each
with a styrofoam latte in her hand
are walking east along College Street
between the police station and Fran's.

They look so cute I can't resist smiling,
even saying, as I pass, "You look so cute!"
Then I turn around and all three of them
have turned around and are facing me.
Two were insulted but the other wasn't.

My fifty-fifth spring offers the illusion
that the pleasure of living more than compensates
for all the suffering and pain and ignorance
and therefore makes one's eye turn to the highly
improbable possibility of love.

Lucky me! I've had fifty-five of them!
And next year I might just have another.
You catch my drift and you know I'm smiling.
But mostly I just want to hang around
with old guys like myself and others.

But then at the northeast corner of Wellesley
and University I get knocked down
by a car turning right—my lights went out.
People are helping me up and screaming at
the stupid driver for being all over the road.

The fall hurt me more than did the car
after being hit with fifty-five springs.
I have a desire to make a sacred sacrifice.
I know—I'll sacrifice my ethnicity.
I never really believed in it anyway.

From now on I'm principally a member
of the human race, all men and women
are my brothers sisters fathers mothers
even the guy who knocked me down with a ton
of metal (his car) and softly I blank out.

I fall into the flowers feeling for fractures.
And finally I find my focal point—
a shadow in the sunshine by the statue
of Alfred W. Purdy in Queen's Park
and I sit there reading for an hour or two.

I'm finishing off *The Guermantes Way*
and especially interesting is the scene
where Monsieur Marcel, because of a few flakes,
brings his great galoshes to the soirée,
and everyone is smirking and guffawing.

You're all set, in case of an arctic blizzard,
they're saying. But there won't be more snow
this evening because they've sprinkled salt
on all the streets. And Madame de Guermantes
is showing off her "magnificent rubies."

They're a little too big for her liking,
too much like a pair of claret glasses
filled to the brim. But so much for that—
I missed you so much through the long winter
and now it's spring I know you won't be back.

Baudelaire-like

I'm no longer miserable, I can scarcely
remember how miserable I used to be
when you abandoned me for another,
some idiotic professor of economics
whom I've known for years and never liked.

He looks like a corpse, he's grey as lead,
and he has an irritating voice
and his mouth is open like an O
resembling an amoeba forever floating.
But if you like him he must be okay.

It would have been kinder if you'd taken
up with some guy I didn't know.
Then I wouldn't have to spend the winter
involuntarily visualizing you both.
All the ways we used to be together.

But never again that's for bloody sure.
I'm forcing myself to believe this really happened.
Pain's strange. You know it when you feel it.
You're being burned with a knife in your heart
and you know you're going to suffer more.

But in the meantime you can't remember
what it was like and you don't believe it.
How silly to love exclusively
when one can love everyone! Billie's birth.
"When It Rains in Here It's Storming at Sea."

Billie was born at the moment a small
earthquake rocked Baltimore for instance.
The only damage was the church steeple
which fell off and landed right side up
in the flower garden. And so it stayed.

The superstitious civic elite shuddered,
and one brave soul said, "If the Lord wanted
that steeple there let us leave it there."
And someone else said, "Let's build a little
fence around it," which they duly did.

Billie was a very powerful person.
She had the knack of being nasty without
being nasty. If you weren't nice to her
she had ways to let you know. She told the tale
of when she was sitting on her granny's lap.

With granny's arms around her, there she slept
and when she woke up granny was dead.
Rigor mortis began to take its toll.
They broke granny's arms to get Billie out.
In poetry we don't tell you what to think.

Billie called Count Basie "Bill" and Basie
called her "William." If you handed her
a joint between sets she'd call a cab
and get him to drive around a corner or two.
Billie's miracles were always happening.

Like a brilliant poet who can't converse,
Billie's voice was different from her speech
and her voice different from her rehearsals.
She was one artist who was not anticipating
posthumous fame. It wouldn't occur to her.

51. Wet-Mopping the Stairs

When I climb to my fifth-floor office
there is often a thin, skinny woman
busy wet-mopping the stairs. I always
give her my cheeriest and most melodious
"Good morning!" but to date she has always been
unpleasant in response. And all she says
is basically "Grumble, grumble," and she
lifts her eyes for a brief moment to scowl.

In the washroom once when she began
pulling on the door to open it
because she had to wet-mop the floor,
"Occupied," I called out in my most
pleasant manner. "Oggyupied, bah,
grumble, grumble, bah!" she replied.

But today as I started up the first
flight, there she was mopping away.

"Good morning!" I sang out sweetly, as always.
She had her back bent over her pail
and as I looked down she was actually smiling
at me, and a nice little smile it was.

"Erk," she said, without a hint of grumbling.
I felt a great surge of happiness.
I suspect I've finally won her over.

52. Mr. Wilson Is Dead

Out of all the friends I've ever had,
whose untimely death would shock me most?
I would have said Bill Mykes straightaway,
or Billy Hay and also Greg Curnoe.
And Bobby Zambori and maybe Brian Longworth.
And those are the ones who up and died.

The good ones die, the bad ones go forever.
I heard a voice in my head above my right ear
saying, "This is Howard Jackson's birthday."
Half an hour later another voice
in the centre of my head said—

"Mr. Wilson's dead." Who's Howard Jackson?
And who the holy heck is Mr. Wilson?

53. Greg Curnoe Is Dead

Greg's death was a huge event in his life.
I'm over the shock but it has changed me.
I'm no longer interested in anything
but raw energy—as in where did all
his go to? All I can listen to
now is mindless music—and I can't
bear to look at a daily paper.

I just read books like Mailer's *On God*
or *The Book of Negroes* or *Havana Nocturne*.

54. Frank Davey Isn't Dead

I don't know beans about literary theory.
What should I read for an overview?
Early Barthes? Someone who wrote about him?
Would Linda still be reading cartons of novels?

I never read as much as Linda did.
A young woman took one look at me
having a drink and said, "You're peaceful but
one day you're going to explode."

It must have been somewhat truthful or
I wouldn't have remembered it all these years.
I'll say we live in a neuro-chemical age
where there's no room for pain or fame.

There are numerous drugs for both. Dig in.
Tell your doctor you want to be all better.
Intellectual pleasure is usually not
denigrated with the word *hedonism*.

Someone made the keen observation
that one can get blown away by a book
at age twenty or even ninety-eight.
George Bowering still reads Kerouac.

One must keep reading challenging books.
You might be harder to please, but still you get
pleasure from the widest range of stuff
even if they're not always up to snuff.

"I'm haunted by the women in Henry James' novels
as if they were alive. Not women I've known,
but as women I've been in the past and the future."
I don't know why, I don't know why, I don't know.

55. Hailstones

A hailstorm. It's too lonely here.
I had no one to watch the hailstones with.
Come home, my darling. Life is sad and serious.

56. World's Biggest Book

I ran into Wally and he proudly
showed me his new book, having just
nicked it at the World's Biggest Bookstore.
What a guy. I'd never have the nerve.

Through those turnstiles with an unpaid book.
Which he often does apparently.
Before the thief alert starts its buzzing
he's off at the speed of a Great Dane.

I reminded him it was I who recommended
that his next book be about his dogs.
Hope you don't mind. Haven't bought the book,
since I'm still reading *The Magic Mountain*.

And for strategic reasons I should finish it
before reading your book, small though it is.
Speaking of Thomas Mann, I think I was
thinking how Wally used to think.

Wally said he couldn't understand
when people say that time goes faster
when one gets older. For him it continues
at the same speed as it does forever.

"Excursus on the Sense of Time," which is
the second section of *The Magic Mountain*,
deals with this whole matter in a more
thorough way than I've seen before.

If Wally were here I'd be urging him
to read it. Maybe I'll read it aloud.
In ancient Japan if you wanted to speak
to the departed you hollered down a well.

Of course Wally wouldn't be interested
in time (in his new state) (was he ever?).
(But he should know filching a book is wrong.)

57. December Celebrations

More travel plans. You probably haven't received
the letter I wrote to you way back in December
and here's another. You may regret giving
me your address. (Really, no, not at all.)
I trust you made it through the celebrations.

I spent a quiet evening with a friend
who was broken up about her relationship.
We watched *Moll Flanders* and we talked and talked
and had a glass of scotch. Not really festive,
but comfy in a slightly awkward way.

This year has been good to me so far.
In the fall, I applied for a couple of jobs.
I got a call yesterday from an embarrassed
director of the university.
She was embarrassed but I was really happy.

For somehow she had misplaced my application.
They've been interviewing, but they haven't
filled the position. She's going to send me
info about their library and law school
and then we'll do a telephone interview.

I don't care about the outcome but
I love the tension it creates. I'm not
keen to move to the U.S.A.,
but there are so few opportunities
for law librarians in Canada.

It's been next to impossible to get
through to Canadian Airlines. I suppose
it's because of the nasty west-coast weather.
Today I persevered and rashly booked
a flight to Rome. Is a month too long?

I'll have to think about it. I have three
weeks to change my mind, but the flights
(for users of points) are nearly full
and low-season travel must be completed
by the thirtieth of April. Convenient?

If you're interested in sharing Italy
I can change the dates within the constraints
of April, or go later and save my points.
You're likely not up to thinking about
travelling with a stranger at this time.

On the other hand, I could visit you
in Nanaimo if you haven't moved by then.
I'm told the flight goes through Vancouver
so I could return from Italy earlier than
planned, and relate my adventures to you.

I just have to return to Ottawa
by April 30 if I'm going to make
use of the "free" flight. I hope that you
don't find these ideas impertinent.
I cannot really anticipate your questions.

58. A Month in Rome

Have I said everything? That's a good
sign-off line. I must remember to use it.
It's amazing how intimate you get on e-mail.
She wants to go with me to Rome for a month.

I couldn't do that without having met her.
So she went alone, phoned me from there,
sent me tons of postcards, and when she was
changing planes at Pearson I went to the airport.

She said my visit filled her full of joy.
Who isn't susceptible, you can't ignore it.
Man was not made to live forever.
She liked my hug. She's very proper and nice.

She says if ever I want to stop writing
just tell me. I'd hate to be waiting for years.
We had about fifteen minutes together
and I quite liked her. She's really nice!

There's many a mystery about love
but we get so exasperated with others.
She wants to take me on a scenic tour
but I've always been a cautious person.

My brother has a wonderful girlfriend.
She's a biochemist, she's dynamite.
She's reserved, but dying to step out.
She wants to be "uprooted completely."

Also she's a concert singer. They did
Fauré's *Requiem* last week at Roy Thomson
and I had a free ticket but couldn't go.
Romance is breaking up that gang of mine.

Guy to God: "What's ten thousand years for you?"
"One second." Guy says: "What's a million dollars
for you?" God says: "A penny." Guy says:
"Give me a million dollars." God says: "Right away!"

My brother is the John Carradine type.
Anyone tell you that? I used to sport
the Jack Nicholson look but it only lasted
for about a year. There's a lot of photos.

Did you ever see Jack in *Witches of Eastwick*?
What a great movie, though it gets a bit
embarrassing at times. I'm the only one
I know who tries to write like John Updike.

Nobody else has quite got it yet.
This is turning tables on an essay.
It's 4:30 in the morning. I'm going to
send this to you before it's too late.

I don't have many close friends. I'm a guy
who doesn't maintain friendships very well
over periods of absence, generally.
A sad story and a literary problem.

It causes my life to have a great number
of ephemeral characters
that come truly alive. The literary problem
is always what to think about in writing.

59. Prelude to a Kiss

Jesus in the clouds over England
in the mushrooms of whatsoever—
the back of my head a computer
of many metaphysical encounters,
by the guides of the toadstools of Norwich.

And York, of my sandwich on rye,
we're leaving Bristol, heading west to Swansea,
of the heavenly wish to tell you I
love you and you are my son of whom
no establishment marblehead tofu.

"I Am the Metastudy" of humanity
on the bogs of Salisbury and the
meteors smashing into Jupiter.
We're caged in the enthusiasm of townships.
Also the technology of themes.

In the darkness over Connemara
you will return to Italy eventually
but again I will never be compelled.
God sends his love from far above
our petty concerns for you are my love.

You have my blessings. So bless anyone
because you are blessed. Wherever you
go, your friends will be waiting for you,
and your mother and I will be with you,
and there will be no need to be afraid.

After pulling the chain how does one
stop the toilet from flushing? Typography
was the style and so they named their daughter
Caslon. Once they overheard her saying,
"I'm named after a typeface and you're not."

60. Know Awareness Knot

The happy community of my dreams
loves to hand out highly publicized
medals to heroes who made a difference—
especially the ones who did it for love
rather than nicer sorts of things.

Ah, your cartoon eyes. I could never
remember which of them was twisted.
You used to say I shouldn't be married
(I'm too much of a loner, you would say)
(somewhere writing juicy poetry).

In eternal recurrence all the souls
get to play all the timeless roles.
A sort of everyday benign possession.
Sometime consciousness will invade
a life system such as you, my dear.

The old soul will refuse to leave
and terrible fights would likely occur
which would be trouble for your flute.
And have you ever repaired a double bass?
You would have two for the price of one.

"Awareness Now," said the T-bone shirt
worn by the lady of abstracted gaze.
But one is not necessarily a passive
observer, only one can contribute
dropping hints from the minds of others.

They'll advise you to get a medical.
Have that throat tumour taken care of.
It's time to quit fooling around with verse.
It's time to change your life drastically
if you haven't been doing it every day.

For even an insignificant length of time
for punctuation to increase ambiguity
as a demonstration of sleight of hand.
Syriax is noted for its doctrine
of angels hovering over the *Globe and Mail*.

In an old suit, greasy shirt and tie,
wearing reading glasses—as old Uncle
Faustus used to say, no dame ever faked
sex with me, I'm a sensitive man.
Maybe it's time to get this over with.

61. Facts of Foolish Blood

In a moment outside time your heart's
bursting and I'm catching spurting blood
in a golden bowl—or maybe not?
We do it a lot, a knife in every eye.
Only Christians go to heaven, they say.

We have arrived, you and I, and so
there can be no more doubt, and now
how can we return in historic time
where we exist factual and blameless.
I don't mind telling you, it's a true fact.

In fact I like to tell it because if
I weren't telling you I'd always be
telling it to myself. But I'm a fool.
It'll make life ever so interesting
for these western smudge-pot bohemians.

62. Never Been to War

Through his telescope he looks out the window

and watches the widows far and wide.
He seems to be examining their techniques—

what they take and what they leave behind.
This will cut down on his learning curve.
When he finds himself completely homeless

he'll know there's absolutely nothing to it.
He was in a pub the other day
and a woman came up to him and said,
"You look like you've never been to war."

63. Subtle Inspections

Nothing will paralyze someone's will
more quickly than wanting to do the thing
nobody else has done, poetry subtlety.
Even when subtlety is submerged
for the lovely pleasure of the few.

Everything we hate is nasty business.
This government is something we dislike.
Out of control? You bet. Every time
they fail to admire my terrible beauty
because of anything you can think of doing.

We seem to have a lot of people already
doing it though not necessarily with style—
or the style that you have had in mind.
For any artist is a foe of culture—
if they can't maintain distance from it.

Alienated from human culture? You bet.
The more we fade out the more we resonate.
Everything you do features the things
we can't do because they're dangerous.
Drink Perrier. Then let's dry off.

Another favourite. Breathe all you can.
Sunbathe too. We walked a thousand miles
out of that dense forest only to be
told we can't sunbathe, make love with strangers
or get our subtle inspections at the terminal.

64. Colette

I can be great friends with someone, then
go away for an alarming number of decades,
and then they're not friends anymore.
That's the way it goes for me. I think
I'm a little tiresome as a person.

It's okay to be serious now and then.
Serious is a realistic thing to be.
I'm listening to the news from different countries—
Finland, Sweden, Netherlands, Pogo.
The latter has an alligator on its flag.

Big stories they would be in Canada
but we hear little about Ireland
or even Howland Owl or Churchy LaFemme,
Beauregard Bugleboy and Porky Pine.
That Colette was a really good writer.

65. Beautiful Words

She's a poet and there's a ton of poetry
in her work, we need her beautiful words.
She writes anonymously about nature
and animals, and so much so that humans
don't seem dominant but of course they are.

Dominant, definitive and lots
of poignancy. She's not an ambitious writer.
She knows she doesn't have to work very hard.
Like Jean Rhys, if that's not condescending
which it's not meant to be. It's reasonable.

To be an artist is something no one can do
except for the one who's doing it.
My formula for determining Doris Lessing
will be an artifact, or maybe not,
of art and discovering dedication.

66. Good Connections

For my purpose I am purposeful.
I mean an individual practitioner,
I focus on the solitary artist,
alone, composed in his composition.
Imagine the first poet to write a poem.

I'm always trying to find an ideal way
of life and love, utterly inescapable,
even though other things must be done
(I assume everybody's the same)
before we open up the watchful sewage.

With good connections our Muse takes me all
over the township as much as I can handle.
She whispers words of wisdom in my wishbone.
She's the invisible and the simple ecstasy
that exists more or less in the things we do.

This is my creed. I simply have to endure.
This simple ecstasy will never die,
though it's not necessary to be true.
You're the humanist atheistic type.
They get old then get smart and get dumb.

67. Lady in White

Let's make lovely suggestions for interesting
things to do and see. The angels, as we
were saying, have the world's sexiest voices.
Fascinated by time and space, yes,
but do not have to suffer living in either.

They can stay in eternity all they want
but many will take an interest in our lives.
Eternity's in love (Blake knew that)
with the products of time. Maybe he
was a previous Greek in an ancient life.

Lucky you never complained of the lack
of seriousness in the letters I write.
Have I said everything? Lady in white?
Having reached space on a certain page
fiery chunks are landing on my nose.

Is this Margaret Drabble's *The Radiant Way*?
It was a hit on my block when it came out.
It's all about three female friends in their
mid-forties and it's set with flashbacks
and flashfronts too of course, in the eighties.

Liz is a shrink, Alix a social worker,
Esther an art historian with a special
interest in Italy. I would like
to propose a name for what will be left
of what is now called this and that.

Canada following the separation
of Manitoba and the elimination
of public funding of the arts and so on,
social services and public transit—
the CBC and the BCB.

And Territories too of the Western
and Eastern Sections of the Northern Part
of North America. The UPTWESNPNA.
A bit too cumbersome? For short we could
call it the United States of America.

68. Happy Moments

By now, according to my celestial informants,
Princess Diana and Mother Teresa are
sitting on a cloud, chatting about time
and eternity, joy, sorrow, love and hate—

while little angels with iPhones float by
taking photographs of the two of them.

69. Slowly Beloved

Aircrafts crashing everywhere you look.

Even dirigibles are colliding in flames.
I'm sitting watching like a little Buddha.

And it's like I'm dying one more time.
Everything is falling very slowly.
You never know what's going to fall next.

Nobody's really panicking apparently.
But someone now and then almost panics.
All day there's been an air of melancholy
which eases the slowness and the sadness.

70. Insatiability

Overheard in front of the orthopedic
hospital on Whisper Street: "I don't
have a single solitary friend
who doesn't have problems with punctuality."

The way zero tolerance policies are
becoming ever more popular
baseball commissioners are thinking of
changing the rules to one strike and you're out.

Overheard on Whisper Street near Jarvis
Collegiate: "I never talk to anyone
below grade ten or maybe nine."
"What a nasty person you've become."

Bev Butler, of St. Mary's, Newfoundland,
is a fish-plant worker who returned
to school at fifty to learn computers.
Scale a codfish and you can a keyboard.

(After work, she says, I used to go to
play darts, now I go to high school.)

71. Skin Diver

You're sitting on the dock of the bay
but you're not working hard enough
on your novel, and as punishment
a random chapter will be now tossed out.

Once you were a leaf that the wind did blow
and that wind really knew how to dance
yet still we hear the Morning Star gently
calling for you all the way to France.

72. Ground Still

On a quiet country lane with the fullness
of the moon rising I tried to create
a sense of silent stillness but couldn't do it.

Nor could I get the water in my bathtub
to be still, at least when I was in it.
Like the differences between you and me.

Stillness and silence are abstractions
and when sprinkled on the *salata caprese*
of life make its taste almost bearable.

73. Sense of Place

There's a place to which each returns
every few years speechless and silent—
like this big bang we return to
every twenty-five billion years.

Who's counting in eternity?
Somewhere there's a sea so wet and vast
each little wave's a twisted universe,
each droplet a million galaxies.

Everyone talks about free will
but I hate it when I slip on horse manure.

74. Melancholy Smiles

Frozen pellets leap from the pavement
like maggots when you fry them in grease,
but you were in the arms of another
and I watched in a state of unease.

The woman you love appears in the paper
and she's in the arms of her famous
and very successful husband and they
both have delirious smiles on their faces.

Whose picture is that? It's Mr. and Mrs.
Nobody. And you're not in love.
Heavens no. I was just saying
if I was in love today I'd be sad.

75. Workout at the Why

The former journalist

Why go on?

Why head on here?

Why proceed on there?

Why knock on any door whenever you want?

Why wiener on wherever there's a western vista?

Why feel good about yourself when there's nowhere to go?

Why fail to notice when there's no horse to wrestle to the ground?

Why scrutinize the sky when it's full of harmless but unnecessary safeguards?

Why not continue when the streets are full of people screaming?

Why inquire about insinuations when all we're interested in is eating bananas?

Why be terrified when there are so many levels to vaporize?

Why go home when you could stay—if you're interested?

Why take an interest in saying no to a free lifetime supply of anything?

Why swim in dirty water if you could be ridiculed for thinking twice?

Why think deep thoughts if you could be treated in Tofino for shock?

Why get raped and beaten by gangs of unemployed fishermen if you can't outscale the opposition?

Why be nasty if there are no more male bastions in your homeland?

Why fornicate with your aunt and uncle now that offshore shopping has been terminated?

Why play the piano if you experience vertigo in the superabundance department?

Why force yourself to regurgitate whatever you want?

Why fear people who are part of a captive market?

Why not supplement your diet with meddlesome instruction manuals?

Why do the majority of men who wear Eau Sauvage
complain to smooth-talking bartenders when they
keep losing money in the jukebox?

Why worry about your failing memory when the great
Buddha in the sky won't allow you to forget anything
he wants you to remember?

Why should the jackpot be bigger just because there were
no winners last time?

Why not sit down and tell me how you got to be so
thoughtful?

Why collect postage stamps when you could take broken
laundromats to the dump?

Why say you're jealous when you're really not?

Why do the nicest people always hang around the bounds
of bad taste?

Why do people with severe melanomas take an interest in
cheap labour?

76. Clothes Peg

Communication leads to living together.
Alternate energy leads to happiness.
A scrubdown each day keeps everything cosy.

I'm trying to get away from the Internet.
I always knew the tried and true won't do.
It's a lovely world but it's a rotten planet.

77. Plenty of Viruses

Every time it rains it rains poets
who have written a wonderful poem today
only to discover that it's identical
to one that was published in *Sweet Tweet*.

Painters who found that working for television
gave them all the freedom they really needed.
Don't you know each cloud contains the souls
of everybody who has ever suffered—

You had a seizure while carving a pumpkin.
So when you hear numerous glasses of beer
shatter on the floor don't look up.
It's your waitress who has slipped on the stairs.

There'll be plenty of pumpkins for everyone.
It's not all that funny anymore.

78. Stiff Elvis and a Pair of Sevens

No paraphernalia is too esteemed
not to be denigrated, for every window's
an opportunity to spy on our colleagues.
Jesus had no appetite for divinity
or the thrills and sweetness of desire.
Orangemen march, it's true, but if you were
orange perhaps you would go marching too.

A little thought for me, it's time to start
eliminating thinking of myself.
But you look great in jeans, and I mean it.
As Elvis said, let ghosts have the right of way
and the dead bury all the stiffs they can find.
Instead of snitching my pair of blue suede shoes
I'll allow people to pay to step on them.

79. Window of Attractiveness

Every window is an opportunity
for observing the widows from every window—
vast and various, like chinks in the wall.
We're all condemned to walk around and think.
That this is so is sincerely self-evident.
You swear by each ripening cubicle and
widows tend to eliminate every window—

Your every window of attractiveness
is an exit for thousands of passionate glances,
withholds every attempt at the soul without.
Understandable doubts about a window
of self-deceits—a bulimia of spectacle
will rage through the windows of the unfortunate
and if it won't we'll make sure it does next time.

80. It's Not Funny Anymore

There's no aces in my deck.
There's no biscuits in my bowl.
There's no conquistadors on my continent.
There's no dragon in my den.
There's no ease in my delivery.
There's no fizz in my fandango.
There's no gate in my fence.
There's no housewife in my hovel and furthermore
There's no heaven in my vocabulary.

There's no ice cream in my freezer.
There's no juice in my red-hot blender.
There's no ketchup on my french fries.
There's no limousine waiting for me.
There's no mustard on my hot dog and I also just noticed that
There's no monkey in my tree.

There's nothing nice about my knobby knee.
There's no over in my underwear.
There's seldom any prisoner in my cell.
There's very little quiet in my quintessence.
There's no rhododendrons in my rock garden.
There's no stallion in any of my stables.
There's no talcum powder on my tray.
There's no umbrella in my understanding.
There's no violin in my orchestra.
There's no water not even in my bathtub.
There's no xylophone under my Xmas tree.
There's no yarmulka in my youth and I'd just like to say
There's hardly any zither in my Zen.

81. Christians Go to Heaven

It's now the appointed hour for you to stop
writing poems and spend the rest of your life
setting all your loveliest poems to music.
Am I telling you what to do? No way.
We will leave that for the Reform Party—
huge billboards all over Alberta saying
REFORM—(I used to belong but I reformed).
After all, only Christians go to heaven.

What a pest that Cheston Sharper can be.
He's cool though. He says he's glad his party
has finally (re)formed the opposition
because now in the question period
he manages to annoy everybody
and this will make life even more boring.

82. Enemy of Culture

Nothing will paralyze somebody's will
more quickly than wanting to do what nobody
else has done because just about anything
you can think of doing has a lot of people
already doing it though not necessarily
with the style you had in mind for all
artists are enemies of culture.

If they're not they had better be.
We'll fade out if we maintain a distance.
If we are alienated from human culture
just think of all the resonance we will have.
And there are things we can't do because
of the danger—and so drink distilled water
and breathe beautiful air and bathe in the sun.

83. The Few Who Flew

How do western separatists create a job?
And fanatic right-wing nihilists who want
the government out of everything they dislike
or in the case of poetry gun control
what they like is nothing if not subtle
even when subtlety is submerged
for the pleasure of the few who flew
out of ten thousand miles of forest.

We walked ten thousand miles out of those
tiny trees only to be told we can't
sunbathe anymore. Make love with buzz saws.
I'll have to bring my forest back tomorrow.

84. Dog Bone

We have arrived, where there can be no doubt,
where we can never return, pointless history,
where we exist as blameless as toast and jam.
I don't mind asking you not to eat ham.
I'm warm but I like to warn because
warning you would be like warning myself—
I do that a lot, a desire in each eye.
We're bound for Benares to be born.

When I was young I desperately desired
much attention and enduring fame.
Today, wanting only to be somewhat
invisible or maybe even more so.
Thinking anything if nothing else.
A tip for anyone on a regular day.

85. Notebook Taking

On a spring day, the street-level windows
at Club 501 were open and a
young fellow was saying, "I'm a young fellow
and I'm strolling along with love in my heart."

Keep your ears open or maybe not.
In front of one of the finest bookstores
one school kid said to another,
"Never associate with younger kids...

"If I were in your shoes I'd have to have
eyes at the back of my head," he said.
This sort of thing happens all the time,
at least it seems to happen every day.

86. Ghosts Float

Winter is coming in, and every day
seems colder than the previous one.
I'm busy rearranging the books
on my shelves from alphabetical
to chronological (the new order).

Ghosts float above the moonlit treetops.
The old Chinese man was chatting with
twenty-two terribly tall Torontonians
in a language I didn't recognize.
He said he was from the Philippines.

The old Chinese man took me aside
and said, "These guys are from Panama.
We're speaking Spanish." How did he know
that I'd been wondering which language they were
chatting in—Spanish or something similar.

Someone told me the number nine is magic.
The flamingo's nose is on the underside
of its beak. They're easily frightened.
Easily frightened people seldom have
nightmares, or so I've been told.

The Chinese man must have been very clever
for he said he could speak Cantonese,
Mandarin, Filipino and Spanish.
And he started learning Japanese
as a young man but he gave it up.

He said Spanish verbs are very hard.
I phoned my old friend Terry whom I hadn't
seen in ten years because he'd moved
to Powell River. He was very surprised
to hear from me. Wouldn't you be?

He had a new wife and a new truck
for hauling wood chips from the saw mill
to the pulp mill. The ambiguity
is not intentional. He said he had
developed a relationship with Jesus.

I told Terry his voice had deepened and
reminded me a lot of his father's.
He was surprised that I could remember
his father's voice after all these years.
His father died in 1959.

Twenty years later Geraldine
Sinclair introduced me to Audrey Thomas.
And Robin Blaser jumped to the stage
calling the people who had been heckling
my friend Victor Coleman "limp dicks."

Terry said his sister, Little Lavarre,
had three children and lived in Calgary.
And his mother, Hilda, married a retired
policeman and settled in the tiny
town of Rosetown, Saskatchewan.

87. A Pint of Guinness

Now that I'm back in Canada I see
that someday I might return to Ireland
but I'll probably never see Petunia again.
I left her awkwardly and sadly and
we didn't even exchange addresses.

I've also been thinking a lot about
the two halves of my journey through Ireland—
the half with Petunia and the half with not.
Each had its moments—with neither heartlessness
nor mindlessness, but care and responsibility.

I'll live in sorrow for the rest of my life
because of my foolishness in earlier years.
And because the gods will eventually
get around to punish every crime.
Life is a pipe, a pint and a fire.

An Irishman would walk over a dozen
naked women for a pint of Guinness.
My fire is like a red red rose that's newly
sprung in June. So leave a message at
the sweetest sound that sweetly plays in tune.

88. Salmon Arm Motor Hotel

I have the right to perform my duties,
one of which is to answer the bell.
Please let me answer the bell for it's
my job to answer every gong or dingdong.

I have the right to sit at the window
with my binoculars and look at the stars
and other mysterious lights in the sky.
It's always my job to wonder and watch.

The only money that's worth having
is money that comes unexpectedly.
Cheques in the mail from anonymous donors
who profess to admire you from afar.

The only gifts worth having, it seems,
are those that accrue without effort.
Our houses are set far from the road
amid gardens of natural beauty.

It seems that we have apprehended all
the world's coldness and none of its poetry.

89. The Nuclear Physicist

In a semi-prosperous neighbourhood
south of the Salvador Allende Hospital
I met a man who claimed to have spent five years
in Moscow studying nuclear physics.
When he returned he was given a professorship
at the University of Havana.

He was a sweet little guy, pleasant, sociable—
and he looked a bit like Garcia Lorca.
He had a 1959 Oldsmobile
and a garage full of parts maintained with care.
He bought a spacious house and married a student
who later became an industrial engineer.

But he was fired because as he said
it was determined by a review committee
that he had too many foreign friends.
So in November he's leaving his house and car
behind and moving to Santo Domingo—
from there it will be easy to get to Miami.

He denies he is being unpatriotic.
He says one can love his country and hate
the system that has it enslaved.
He says that Fidel thinks *he's* the country.
It's the ancient *l'état c'est moi* syndrome.
A lot of people in Havana talk like this.

Later I tell the story of the physicist
to René Caparros, a dedicated supporter
of the Revolution and he takes me
on a tour of the old seventeenth-century
Convento de Santa Clara at Calle Cuba
where they're responsible for restorations.

Restoration is slow but a lot has been done.
There are three students busily involved
in restoring ancient silverware.
René has met Fidel several times.
It's intimidating to be in his presence.
A revolution can't be totally perfect.

People say only ten per cent support Fidel.
René is one but those who support Fidel
somehow don't sound terribly convincing
and they aren't as passionate as others.
And when they speak about the Revolution
they have memorized what they're going to say.

90. Cowboy Boots

There was truth in what she said about me
being a megalomaniac because of my cowboy
boots and being pompous because of my middle
initial. Should I throw myself at her feet
and shed true tears and plead for forgiveness?

She tells me I'm a terrible totalitarian
because I can't face the world without
putting on a lousy pair of boots.
I think maybe she doesn't really love me.
And I don't really love her probably.

I'm back to wearing Rockports but I still
have that middle initial. I'm even eating
low-fat tofu vegetarian pepperoni—
and I only wore those boots for about
two days and only to be an inch taller.

91. Dylan Is Helping Me

The Other World is out. It's a lovely book,
full of charmingly deep childhood dreams.
This guy is fantastic. I can't wait
to meet him again and maybe he'll come to town
for the fall launch. I'll have to insist.

He said to me once, "I don't care
about my roots and I don't care about
anyone else's roots." We were shooting
pool at the time, and everyone was
checking him out because he was so cute.

He loved the Rodney Dangerfield joke where Rodney's
in the hot tub with a bunch of co-eds.
He says to one of them, what's your major?
Nineteenth-century American poetry—why?
I need help with straightening out my Longfellow.

But this is not a joke. It's about a fellow
who used to operate a wonderful restaurant
and then he was in a horrible car accident.
It's terribly depressing being around him.
He has severe brain damage, and he slobbers.

But though he can't talk he's always cheery.
He can't drink fluids, so you have to mix
a solidifying powder in his orange juice.
And there are all these photos around to show
how he used to look before the crash.

His wife from whom he was separated
at the time of the accident, dropped everything
and is devoting her life to caring for him.
He types things on his little computer
such as "I think Dylan is helping me."

Did he mean Bob Dylan or Dylan Thomas?
It turned out Dylan was his brother
who died of AIDS last year. And he says
this a hundred times a day, that he thinks
Dylan is helping him from the other world.

The sense of love and devotion is staggering
and ultimately sobering as well.
It made me feel like a lesser being.
It's hard to imagine what life would be like
if this happened to my daughter or brother.

92. Pepe El Romano

Are we finished? I can't believe we are.
It's all over for another year.
How wonderful! And how fortunate
we were to have such passionate students.
I think we did a great job all around.

Do you mind if we pat ourselves
on the back firmly and then let out
a great sigh of relief. And we did good.
As good as anyone could do. There's a little
review of *Musgrave's Landing* in *Venue*.

It's available in Sidney at Tanner's Books.
Also at the Resthaven Grocery.
This review will make you feel so fine
all over, guaranteed. There's also a
little story by me in the same issue.

There are two pictures, one of me
smiling, and of course one is frowning.
And maybe I'll send copies of this note
to our friends and colleagues so they won't
be deprived of this excellent magazine.

It happens to be published in the office
next to mine. There's no sign on the door
but Margo will be able to zip up
to Saskatoon and get one there
at the United Cigar Store or whatever.

And as for McClusk he can get it at
let's see now oh by golly they don't
have a listing for Owen Sound either.
I'm shocked, appalled and embarrassed too.
I guess the closest one would be Waterloo.

There are numerous places there where
they can get it, the Westmount Place Pharmacy
and of course the Quick Trip Variety.
By the way if we're looking for somebody
next year I'd recommend Guillermo Verdecchio.

He's a poet, a playwright and an actor.
He's fantastic, he's won two Chalmers and
two Governor General's Awards (and deserved them)
for his two plays—*The Noam Chomsky Lectures*
and *Fronteras Americanas*. He lives in Vancouver.

93. I Can't Remember His Name

This Argentinian movie, *Dark Side of the Heart*,
won the best film award at the Festival,
but it gets terrible reviews in Toronto
because it's about a "macho poet" who drops
women if they can't satisfy him.

Personally, I might have wanted to see it
if it were a decade or two ago.
It's directed by Eliseo Subiela
who also directed *Man Facing Southeast*
which I saw without benefit of subtitles.

My poems go leaping from crag to crag
like a stubble-faced crybaby, it's probably
because I've been writing for so long,
forty years of poems to various friends.
It started with a pen pal in New Westminster.

I can't remember his name, but for every
letter he wrote me I wrote a dozen to him.
No wonder he said he couldn't write anymore.
I think I hear my mother calling me,
he said, then he never wrote again.

94. The Waste Land

I never liked arguing in the car.
It made me terribly nervous all the time—
heavy negotiations at high speed—
with a few little angels in the back seat.

I always used to think fast in reverse
trying to figure out what I had said.
A daily occurrence for seventeen years.
Did I tell you I found the Holy Grail?

I'm reading Jessie Weston's *From Ritual to Romance*.
This book got T.S. Eliot to write
The Waste Land. It's well written and provocative.
And clears up stuff and makes a lot of sense.

I didn't like *Sorrows of Young Werther*
or any book with Sorrows in the title.
A guy came up behind me on Yonge Street—
placed his fingers on the small of my back.

And said that I was a terribly sexy man.
He thought it odd to see a man in boots.
I thought of you, I said not where I'm from.
Aklavik, Inuvik and Tuktoyaktuk.

95. Couplets of Desire

Kangaroo jackets. Did you know they make
Australian beer out of all them hops.

Tomorrow my two little friends from Canberra
who have recently moved to Montreal

are in town. My Kiwi friend says I
shouldn't see them, it's not respectable

for a gentleman my age to be hanging
around with a pair of beautiful

women in their early twenties and she's
right of course but what else can I do?

It's not as if there's going be any
hanky panky if you catch my drift

or anything like that. In fact I've already
made it plain to my Tokyo friend

that she is the only one for me and also
we're married already (did I forget?)

for the rest of our lives. Even if she
does live on the other side of the world

I will never ever make love to another
(very silly!) until my dying day

and maybe not then (we had a nice weekend!)
and we also had fun on Wednesday and Thursday.

Besides I have to go in for minor surgery
tomorrow morning at seven-thirty-three.

My repairs are in the zones of extreme intimacy.
I took my New Zealand friend to see *Belle Epoque*

yesterday. Second time I saw it
and the first I ever saw a film twice

while it was still in its first run.
It was even better the second time.

A wonderful movie and the sexiest
film I ever saw, although my New

Zealand friend says she's been watching
some of those British films from the sixties

and they were pretty hot or so she says.
But you really should check out *Belle Epoque*.

It's a great film with echoes of *Smiles of
a Summer Night* and *Some Like It Hot*.

But *Belle Epoque* is transcendental throughout.
The best Spanish-language film of all time.

96. Lucky Binoculars

What luck! Down with a cold in Roma.
Spent the afternoon in bed asleep
and having peculiar Roman hallucinations.
I must have taken the city apart again
and put it back together a thousand times.
The third day we went to the Etruscan Museum
at the Villa Giulia in the Borghese Gardens.
We strolled along past the British Academy
and Romanian, Dutch and Belgian academies.
The murals and wall paintings in the villa
with cupids frolicking in the flowery sunlight.
Pagan innocence, holding a rose to its nose.

A large drinking vessel with two faces,
one on each side. As you drink
you can have either one facing you.
Not unusual but in this case the faces
are of an Etruscan woman on one side
and a lovely African woman on the other,
the paint intact after 2,600 years.

"Hence Genius, born to thrive by interchange
of peace and excitation." (Wordsworth)

The concept of spotlessness is different
in Zen than it is in the Grail legends.
In Zen spotlessness doesn't convey
the notion of sin, freedom from preconceptions.
But I think they are the same. First off, everything
in the Grail legends is metaphorical,
nothing is what it seems. If one is spotless
in the Zen sense then he is free
from ordinary desires and sees the unity

of all life and lacks interest in the norm.
This is how morals and spirituality
became incestuously intertwined.

Lucky I had binoculars and could indulge
birdwatching and other forms of voyeurism.
La Cappella della Madonna di Monseratto.
Wonderful strange legends surrounding it.
Time to think, meditate, scheme and so on.
My daughter would join us in Milano
and we spent eight days together in Florence
before she decided to head for Corfu.
We took little trips to Siena and Pisa
and have been here in Assisi for a week.
Thinking of heading down to Rome for ten
days and back to England and home.
Venice is out of the question in August.
I'm sending a bookmark for that woman
who collects bookmarks. Give my regards.

97. Standing Ovations

Dreamt about Bill Davies here in Assisi,
nineteen years after his death in Hamilton.
The CN Tower was being erected and there
was Bill, looking somewhat like Saint Francis.
He looked at me but no recognition.
A crowd of people were surrounding him.
Last night at the Teatro Comunale Metastasio
the Chamber Music Ensemble was late showing up
so a technically good but overblown pianist
played tons of Beethoven through the years.
The pianist seemed more moved than most
in the audience. A small group, and probably
it seemed they were all friends of the maestro.
They went overboard with the standing ovations.
He kept giving encores with a pleased look
but people were leaving left and right.

After intermission two German tourists
were sitting in our seats so I stood
in front with my arms crossed over my chest.
The tourists were amused. They said, "I guess
this is the British way of doing things."
The chamber music group was wonderful.
Piano, French horn, clarinet, oboe, bassoon.
They played Mozart the way he'd like to be played.

98. A Few Green Leaves

Bellagio was beautiful, my studio
was the belltower of a little used
sixteenth-century chapel deep in the woods
and on a cliff-face overlooking Lake Como
surrounded by wonderfully strange legends.

Finished Barbara Pym's *A Few Green Leaves*,
visited San Damiano and bought and scanned
the British papers. None of the bookstores
has anything by Pietro Metastasio
though they acknowledged he was from Assisi.

Shall we return to Rome? I need stimulation.
I really think I get much more of that
at home than I do in Italy.
Certainly more in England. Getting nostalgic.
Should I head back to England rather than Rome?

And yet, today in the Basilica
the light from the stained-glass windows in
the Magdalene Chapel seemed to penetrate
deeply into the darkness of my heart.
Problems with Italy. I'm having trouble.

I just don't have the knack for languages.
Slow to pick it up. Terrible handicap.
And trouble coping with the infestation
of tourists. German, French, British and so on.
My fondest regards and a thousand warm thoughts.

99. Microscopic Surgery

Going to stay some time before hopping
on the train all the way to Como.
Disoriented in London. It's so warm,
humid, but human, overcast and muggy.
Joy's not well, she got sick in Egypt.

String quartet at St. Dunstan's in Fleet Street.
Violinist cut her finger in a kitchen
accident and hadn't played for a year.
Microscopic surgery. Cut nerve.
But now she thinks she's going to be fine.

After the wine and cheese reception (tacky!)
(but nice) took picture of an old statue
of Queen Elizabeth (the first) that had just
been discovered in somebody's basement
and installed over the sacristy door.

Walking all through Westminster buying slides.
Weatherman on BBC-1:
Today most wet spots will become
dry and most dry spots will become wet.
Of course he said this with a smiling face.

Author's note: *All of these poems were written during the period of 1988 to 1995. They were assembled and revised during the period of 2010 to 2012.*

Acknowledgements

I would like to thank my editor, the poet and novelist Stuart Ross, for his patience, intellect and acumen.

Many thanks to my publisher, Denis De Klerck, for his wisdom and forbearance.

Also B.E. who shared many of these moments.

And most of all my darling Merlin Homer. A thousand kisses.

David W. McFadden began writing poetry in 1956 and began publishing poetry in 1958. *Why Are You So Sad? Selected Poems of David W. McFadden* (Insomniac Press) was shortlisted for the 2008 Griffin Prize for Poetry, and *Be Calm, Honey* (Mansfield Press) was shortlisted for the 2009 Governor General's Award for Poetry (his third such nomination). McFadden is the author of about 30 books of poetry, fiction, and travel writing. He lives in Toronto.

Other Books From Mansfield Press

Poetry

Nelson Ball, *In This Thin Rain*

Stephen Brockwell & Stuart Ross, eds., *Rogue Stimulus: The Stephen Harper Holiday Anthology for a Prorogued Parliament*

Alice Burdick, *Holler*

Gary Michael Dault, *The Milk of Birds*

Pier Giorgio Di Cicco, *Early Works*

Christopher Doda, *Aesthetics Lesson*

Rishma Dunlop, *Lover Through Departure: New and Selected Poems*

Jaime Forsythe, *Sympathy Loophole*

Jason Heroux, *Emergency Hallelujah*

David W. McFadden, *Be Calm, Honey*

Leigh Nash, *Goodbye, Ukulele*

Lillian Necakov, *Hooligans*

Peter Norman, *At the Gates of the Theme Park*

Natasha Nuhanovic, *Stray Dog Embassy*

Catherine Owen & Joe Rosenblatt, with Karen Moe, *Dog*

Jim Smith, *Back Off, Assassin! New & Selected Poems*

Robert Earl Stewart, *Campfire Radio Rhapsody*

Carey Toane, *The Crystal Palace*

Priscila Uppal, *Winter Sport: Poems*

Steve Venright, *Floors of Enduring Beauty*

Fiction

Marianne Apostolides, *The Lucky Child*

Kent Nussey, *A Love Supreme*

Marko Sijan, *Mongrel*

Tom Walmsley, *Dog Eat Rat*

Non-Fiction

George Bowering, *How I Wrote Certain of My Books*

Pier Giorgio Di Cicco, *Municipal Mind*

Amy Lavender Harris, *Imagining Toronto*

For a complete list of Mansfield Press titles, please visit mansfieldpress.net